Set design by John Stark

Photo by John Lamb

A scene from the Mustard Seed Theatre production of *Falling*.

FALLING

BY DEANNA JENT

DRAMATISTS
PLAY SERVICE
INC.

FALLING
Copyright © 2011, Deanna Jent

All Rights Reserved

CAUTION: Professionals and amateurs are hereby warned that performance of FALLING is subject to payment of a royalty. It is fully protected under the copyright laws of the United States of America, and of all countries covered by the International Copyright Union (including the Dominion of Canada and the rest of the British Commonwealth), and of all countries covered by the Pan-American Copyright Convention, the Universal Copyright Convention, the Berne Convention, and of all countries with which the United States has reciprocal copyright relations. All rights, including without limitation professional/amateur stage rights, motion picture, recitation, lecturing, public reading, radio broadcasting, television, video or sound recording, all other forms of mechanical, electronic and digital reproduction, transmission and distribution, such as CD, DVD, the Internet, private and file-sharing networks, information storage and retrieval systems, photocopying, and the rights of translation into foreign languages are strictly reserved. Particular emphasis is placed upon the matter of readings, permission for which must be secured from the Author's agent in writing.

The English language stock and amateur stage performance rights in the United States, its territories, possessions and Canada for FALLING are controlled exclusively by DRAMATISTS PLAY SERVICE, INC., 440 Park Avenue South, New York, NY 10016. No professional or nonprofessional performance of the Play may be given without obtaining in advance the written permission of DRAMATISTS PLAY SERVICE, INC., and paying the requisite fee.

Inquiries concerning all other rights should be addressed to Sendroff & Baruch, LLP, 1500 Broadway, Suite 2201, New York, NY 10036. Attn: Mark Sendroff.

SPECIAL NOTE
Anyone receiving permission to produce FALLING is required to give credit to the Author as sole and exclusive Author of the Play on the title page of all programs distributed in connection with performances of the Play and in all instances in which the title of the Play appears for purposes of advertising, publicizing or otherwise exploiting the Play and/or a production thereof. The name of the Author must appear on a separate line, in which no other name appears, immediately beneath the title and in size of type equal to 50% of the size of the largest, most prominent letter used for the title of the Play. No person, firm or entity may receive credit larger or more prominent than that accorded the Author. The following acknowledgments must appear on the title page in all programs distributed in connection with performances of the Play:

First produced at Mustard Seed Theatre, St. Louis, MO, September 2011.

Subsequently produced by Terry Schnuck, James & Catherine Berges,
Crystal Beuerlein and Michael & Noemi Neidorff
Off-Broadway at the Minetta Lane Theatre, New York City, October 2012.

*This play is dedicated to
the love and lessons learned from my Dad.*

ACKNOWLEDGMENTS

My heartfelt thanks to:

— Jason Sommer and Kim Wylie, who said "write it."

— the original cast, who helped me fix it and brought it to life; the crew who made feathers fly.

— my friend and colleague, Lori Adams, who directed the St. Louis and New York productions.

— Terry Schnuck, for believing.

— Michelle and Leslie, for sharing coffee, laughter and tears.

— my children, Chris, Lindzey and Andy; my siblings and extended family near and far.

— my husband, Steve, for first being my madrigal partner and then my life partner.

PRODUCTION NOTES

Words are chosen and used carefully in this house. The shortest and most direct statements get the best results with Josh, so resist the urge to add anything to "fill the silence."

Avoid sentimentality. Tami and Bill don't feel sorry for themselves — they're simply doing what needs to get done to get through another day (until that becomes impossible).

The key to playing Josh is not to mimic people with autism — it's to discover what inner forces drive Josh's behavior. His almost constant movement feeds his under-reactive nervous system the input to help him maintain balance. His delight in visual stimulation (feathers falling, videos, wheels moving) comes from a need to tune out unwanted noise and to control his visual environment. He plans everything in advance, because surprises are so scary. His frustration with a DVD breaking is not out of love for that particular DVD but because he has an order in which DVDs must be watched, and if he can't watch that one, he can't move on to the next. When scared or stuck, he pushes on his chin because the pressure is calming to him. If the situation escalates and he loses control, he creates all-over pressure on his body and muscles by grabbing and holding tightly whoever is with him. His violent episodes are much like a "melt-down" in a toddler — a period of time in which pure emotion overcomes thought. When the episode is over and thought returns, Josh grieves his actions and lack of control. His violence never comes out of a desire to hurt anyone or anything.

Mostly, the actor playing Josh needs to understand that his mind is constantly busy running scripts of favorite shows, planning future events, taking in each new stimulus in his environment. His inability to communicate does not indicate a lack of intelligence or focus or problem-solving abilities.

Both the original St. Louis and the New York productions held talkbacks after EACH performance. Since the show ran 75–80 minutes, a break became a kind of intermission, and the talkbacks became a sort of second act. Audience reactions varied from anger to gratitude. Some saw their story told truthfully for the first time;

some had no idea this sort of family dynamic existed. I strongly encourage you to plan for talkbacks — it worked well when some of the cast or production team stayed to respond to audience questions and remarks. Below are some talking points you can use at the start of the talkback; these are answers to the most commonly asked questions.

- The playwright has a son with severe autism, very much like Josh. Her son, Andy, was sixteen years old when she wrote the play. The information presented about lack of resources and housing options is true. Efforts are being made on many fronts to address these ongoing issues. (It would be great to have information about your own community resources available.)

- All people with autism are not like Josh. In fact, no two people with autism are quite alike. It's a spectrum disorder and Josh is at the severe end of the spectrum.

- Ultimately, this is not a play about autism, but about Loving Someone who is Hard to Love.

Finally, the best comment I received about the play was this: "Do you know what's wrong with your play? Everybody's right! It's so much easier if someone is wrong."

Make everybody right. Embrace the hard.

Deanna Jent
January 2013

FALLING was developed and produced by Mustard Seed Theatre in St. Louis, Missouri, opening on September 1, 2011. It was directed by Lori Adams; the set design was by John C. Stark; the costume design was by Deanna Jent; the lighting design was by Julie Mack; the sound design was by Zoe Sullivan; movement and combat were by Shaun Sheley; prop design was by Meg Brinkley; the stage manager was Adam Flores; and the assistant stage manager was Jessica Haley. The cast was as follows:

JOSH MARTIN	Jonathan Foster
TAMI MARTIN	Michelle Hand
LISA MARTIN	Katie Donnelly
BILL MARTIN	Greg Johnston
SUE MARTIN	Carmen Russell

FALLING was subsequently produced by Terry Schnuck, James and Catherine Berges, Crystal Beuerlein, and Michael and Noemi Neidorff at the Minetta Lane Theatre in New York City, opening October 15, 2012. Jeffrey Chrzczon was Executive Producer. Casting was by Pat McCorkle. It was directed by Lori Adams; the set design was by John C. Stark; the costume design was by Tristan Raines; the lighting design was by Julie Mack; the sound design was by Raymond Shilke; movement and combat were by Rick Sordelet; prop design was by Zachary Roland; the stage manager was Brian Meister; and the assistant stage manager was Pamela Edington. The cast was as follows:

JOSH MARTIN	Daniel Everidge
TAMI MARTIN	Julia Murney
LISA MARTIN	Jacey Powers
BILL MARTIN	Daniel Pearce
SUE MARTIN	Celia Howard

Adam Donschik, Shannon Koob, Susan Lehman and Jonathan Judge-Russo were the understudies.

CHARACTERS

JOSHUA — Age 18, with severe autism. He is large and strong. Most of the time he is happy, and does what will be referred to as his "happy dance" — big movements of his shoulders, back and forth, accompanied by guttural sounds and smiles and head tilts. He is fascinated by visual stimuli and scared by loud and unexpected noises. He has limited verbal/communication skills.

TAMI — His mother, in her 40s. She and her husband have been trained in behavioral intervention and teaching skills, which is evidenced in how they interact with Josh and sometimes bleeds over into their interaction with others. She sells real estate part-time. Fantasy and alcohol are her stress relievers.

LISA — Age 16, his sister. Wants to be a typical girl in a typical home. Isn't and is frustrated by that. She and her father take yearly summer vacations to visit his mother (Grammy Sue). This is their two-week escape from daily home life. She may deal with her stress by overeating.

BILL — His father. Tries to relieve stress by making jokes — would like to relieve stress by having sex. Neither are working too well for him right now. His job isn't mentioned, but he is a supervisor (mostly office work) at a construction firm.

GRAMMY SUE — Bill's mother. She brings with her the hope that her sincere Christian faith can intervene to help everyone in her son's family. She is genuinely concerned and confused, but she is not a scold. She is in a "boot" because she broke two of her toes a few days prior to this visit.

LAWRENCE — Caseworker for the Department of Child and Family Services, played by the same actor who plays Joshua. This character should be quite different in bearing and speech from Joshua, but there shouldn't be a huge effort to "disguise" the fact that it's the same actor.

SETTING

A living room and dining room. There is a front door and two other exits — one door to the kitchen and a hallway that leads to bedrooms. In one part of the room there is a box rigged with rope and filled with feathers that can be tipped over so they float down on a person's head. An office area contains a computer, many books, some empty food wrappers. There is a hutch and a dining room table that seats four, a couch a coffee table, and a small TV/VCR unit in a corner on the floor. There is a visible calendar on the wall, filled with writing. Videotapes are stacked in exact piles of four around the perimeter of the television space. There may be many trains lined up as well. Every toy has a specific place in Josh's world.

It is March 2011. The play is set in the suburbs of a Midwestern city.

NOTE

The bus safety vest is designed to keep the person wearing it from unbuckling the safety belt and standing up/walking around the bus. It zips in the back and has loops at the shoulders that are linked to loops on the bus seat once the person wearing the vest is seated.

FALLING

Scene One

Joshua enters the room from the hallway/bedrooms. As he walks through the room, he occasionally pulls his shirt partially up exposing a nipple (one of his habits). Josh moves under the feather box, does a short ritual of touching certain things and moving a certain way, and then dumps the feathers on his head. He squeals and is doing his happy dance as Tami enters from the kitchen carrying a laundry basket.

TAMI. Hey, Josh — I like that smile! Remember, feathers go back in box, please. *(She exits to the bedrooms, and Josh begins picking up the feathers and placing them in the box. Tami and Lisa enter, talking. As they walk across the room toward the kitchen, Tami keeps herself always between Lisa and Josh, although this should not call attention to itself. Lisa is brushing her hair as she talks.)*
LISA. ... and so we'll be working on club stuff till 5:30, and then we're going to Lori's to eat and study ...
TAMI. Did you forget that Grammy Sue is flying in this afternoon?
LISA. So?
TAMI. I'm sure she'll want to see you — I thought you'd plan to be home tonight.
LISA. She's gonna be here for a week, right?
TAMI. What do you need to do at Lori's?
LISA. Study and stuff. You told me yesterday I could ... *(And they're in the kitchen. Josh has finished putting the feathers in the box. He does his short ritual and drops them on his head again. He is doing his happy dance as Bill enters from the kitchen with Josh's backpack and bus safety vest. Bill is partially dressed for the day in khakis, a T-shirt and socks. He puts the backpack and vest on the side table by the door.)*

BILL. Feathers back in box please. Bus soon.
JOSH. No bus. No thank you.
BILL. Feathers back in box.
JOSH. No bus.
BILL. Feathers in box. Bus at 7:45. *(Josh makes a fist and pushes on his forehead between his eyes. [This is a stress reliever.] After a moment, he starts picking up the feathers and putting them in the box. Bill moves toward the kitchen as Tami enters, drinking a cup of coffee.)*
TAMI. *(To Bill.)* Smoothie time. *(To Josh.)* Lisa is going to use the blender. We'll do "cover our ears" and then you can pick a game. Ready? *(Josh covers his ears with his hands and crouches. Bill moves to the kitchen door.)* OK Lisa! *(To Josh as he covers his ears.)* Here we go! *(Tami signals Bill and they both start counting down on their fingers — Tami so that Josh can see and Bill so that Lisa can see. A blender runs in the kitchen.)* 10-9-8-7-6-5-4-3-2- *(Bill signals Lisa to stop and the blender noise stops.)* and 1. Noise is all done. *(Josh pulls his hands away from his ears.)* Good job! Now, do you want to do "London Bridge" or "Big Bad Wolf"?
JOSH. *(Excited.)* And blow the house down!
TAMI. Alright! Dad — can you be a big bad wolf? *(Bill joins them. Josh is excited.)* Once upon a time there were three little pigs who went out in the world ...
JOSH. *(Grabbing a finger with each word, hurrying the story along.)* Straw, wood, bricks.
TAMI. OK! Aaaannnd ... So the three pigs were safe in their house of brick when along came the ...
JOSH. *(In a deep but not very loud voice.)* Big Bad Wolf
TAMI. And he said:
BILL. *(In deep voice, which makes Josh laugh.)* "Little pigs, little pigs, let me in."
TAMI. And the pigs said ... *(Cueing Josh.)*
JOSH and TAMI. *(Together. high voices.)* Not by the hair on my chinny-chin-chin
BILL. *(Really getting into it.)* Then I'll huff, and I'll puff, and I'll blow your house in! *(He blows as hard as he can, then he stops.)* Wait a minute, that didn't work! *(Josh nearly wets himself because this is so funny.)* Let me try again. *(He blows and blows, until finally he "passes out.")*
TAMI. And the wolf blew himself out, and the pigs lived ... *(Cueing Josh.)*

JOSH and TAMI. Happy ever after. *(Tami claps and helps Bill back to his feet. Josh is very happy, maybe squealing.)*
TAMI. Yay for "Little Pigs"! Now let's finish picking up feathers. *(Josh resumes putting feathers back in the box. Tami gives a nod to Bill and exits back into the kitchen. Bill helps Josh with the feathers.)*
BILL. When we're finished with feathers, we'll get ready for the bus. *(The following conversation is matter-of-fact from Josh, he's still in a good mood, just stating his version of fact.)*
JOSH. *(Leaving the feathers task.)* No bus.
BILL. Sure there's a bus! It's Thursday, school day.
JOSH. There's no school. No thank you.
BILL. What?
JOSH. No school. School is stuck.
BILL. Bus at 7:45 to take you to school.
JOSH. *(Frowning, louder.)* No school. School is stuck.
BILL. Today's a school day, buddy!
JOSH. *(A strained voice, agitated.)* A school day buddy!
BILL. Do you want to do "Little Pigs" again?
JOSH. No thank you.
BILL. Do you want to watch computers or read a book? *(Josh responds with the fist to forehead. Bill steps back.)*
JOSH. No book. No school. *(He repeats his fist-to-forehead gesture with more force and some angry noises. He begins pacing rapidly as Bill moves away toward the kitchen door and calls out carefully.)*
BILL. Lisa, Tami — I'm getting hungry for some peanut butter, just so you know. *(Josh continues to pace. Bill carefully keeps some distance between them.)*
TAMI. *(From behind the door.)* Do you need some jelly with that?
JOSH. *(As before.)* A school day buddy!
BILL. Not just yet, I'll let you know. *(Bill turns his focus back to Josh. Unseen by him, Tami cracks to door open to watch.)*
JOSH. *(Additional physical agitation.)* School is stuck.
BILL. I hear what you're saying.
JOSH. School is stuck.
BILL. You don't want to go to school.
JOSH. You don't want to go to school
BILL. *(Sign language prompt as he says "I.")* "I don't want to go to school."
JOSH. *(Loud and moving toward Bill.)* I don't want to go to school.

(Tami sees that Josh is moving aggressively toward Bill, so she moves quickly between them, getting Josh's attention and turning him around.)
TAMI. Josh — Mommy has a surprise! Come with me. *(Josh pauses as Tami walks up toward the calendar and Bill backs away from Josh.)* Remember what's on the calendar today? Grammy Sue is coming. And she is bringing a present for you. Come look at the calendar. *(Josh walks up to look at the calendar. He takes Tami's finger and points to the current day.)* See. Grammy Sue after school.
JOSH. *(Grumpily.)* There's no school.
TAMI. *(Cheery but not too loud playful voice.)* Uh-oh! We can't change school days *(Exaggerated with a big gesture.)* Rats!
JOSH. *(Mimicking her gesture and sound.)* Rats!
TAMI. But after school, Grammy Sue will have a present for you.
JOSH. *(After a short pause.)* Birthday.
TAMI. Not birthday. A present because she loves you.
JOSH. Present. *(His agitation has stopped, and he smiles.)* Present! *(Josh moves to where his backpack and safety vest are and holds out his arms for the vest. Tami gets the backpack and Bill put on his safety vest.)*
TAMI. *(As Bill is putting on the vest.)* Grammy is bringing a present and she will be staying here for a few days.
BILL. So after school, when the bus brings you home …
JOSH. No bus.
BILL. After school, when the bus …
JOSH. Bus is gonna late.
TAMI. What?
JOSH. Bus is gonna late.
TAMI. You think the bus is going to be late?
JOSH. Yes. School is broken. *(Bill and Tami exchange looks. Tami steps "into the scene.")*
TAMI. I know you want there to be no school today. But it's Thursday, school day.
JOSH. Bus is gonna late.
TAMI. After school, Grammy has a present for you.
JOSH. No school.
TAMI. Remember, if it's a "safe-hands" day at school, when you get home you get to pick a new marble.
JOSH. Pick a marble.
TAMI. Yes, when you have safe hands at school, then…?
JOSH. Marble.
TAMI. Yes.

JOSH. Marble.

TAMI. Yes. After school. A present AND a marble.

JOSH. *(Looks out the window on the front door, in an animated voice.)* Where is the bus?

TAMI. *(Relieved, this is now part of the regular morning script — in a cheery voice.)* I don't know. Where is the bus?

JOSH. *(Starts keeping time with hand gestures, turns to Tami and takes her hands and beats time as he sings softly.)* "Wheels on the bus go round and round … " *(He waits for Tami to sing her part. Bill joins in with Tami. This is not part of Josh's routine.)*

TAMI and BILL. "Round and round"

JOSH. *(Stops singing abruptly, looks at Bill.)* Dad. Stop singing.

BILL. *(Quickly, not a problem.)* OK. Sorry, buddy.

JOSH. *(To Tami.)* Wheels on the bus go round and round

TAMI. "Round and round."

JOSH. "Round and round." *(Together they sing, going faster and faster.)*

TAMI and JOSH. "Wheels on the bus go round and round all through the town!" *(Josh goes to the front door and opens it, then runs outside.)*

BILL. Do you want me to … *(Tami gestures to Bill's shoeless feet and exits. Bill checks for messages on his phone as Lisa opens the door and peeks in. Bill sees her.)* He's outside waiting for the bus with Mom.

LISA. *(Entering and sipping her smoothie.)* It's not gonna work.

BILL. What?

LISA. Grammy here with him.

BILL. It'll be fine. It's just for a week while they …

LISA. Yeah, but it only takes …

BILL. We're taking care of it.

LISA. Whatever. Does she know to bring her helmet and shield?

BILL. I'm sure she's packed that, along with her teenage sarcasm deflector. *(Lisa shakes her head as she finishes her drink. She takes the glass back into the kitchen. Calling to her.)* Who's picking you up this morning? *(He picks up some empty food wrappers and moves toward the desk.)*

LISA. *(From the kitchen.)* Lori.

BILL. Did you rinse out the blender?

LISA. *(Entering.)* Yes. *(A honk from outside, Lisa grabs her backpack as Bill throws away the food wrappers. As Lisa reaches the front door, it opens, and Tami and Lisa nearly collide.)*

TAMI. Whoa! Look out! *(Lisa exits.)* Bye, Lisa! *(Waits for a response, then closes the door.)*
BILL. *(Moving toward the table.)* So — was he done being our little "Pillsbury NO-boy"? *(They smile at the familiar joke.)*
TAMI. All smiles. Once we get to "Wheels on the Bus" we're good to go. *(Bill nods as Tami crosses toward the computer.)*
BILL. So, uh, I'm a little confused.
TAMI. Oh?
BILL. I thought "peanut butter" meant stay out because he's upset.
TAMI. Yes, but …
BILL. And don't come in until the person says "Jelly."
TAMI. Right, but …
BILL. Because more people coming in escalates the situation.
TAMI. Usually. I just thought of the present thing with Grammy, and I didn't know if you knew it was on the calendar.
BILL. So we have these meetings and set these rules for no reason.
TAMI. No. But I thought you could use some help. There's always exceptions to the rules.
BILL. Sure. But what would you be saying if I had done that to you?
TAMI. I don't know. Maybe "Thank-you for saving my ass"?
BILL. I doubt it. *(Bill shakes his head and exits to finish getting dressed. Tami stands still, taking in the silence. With a big breath, she tries to shake the tension out of her neck and shoulders. She looks at the computer and makes a decision. She clicks an icon. A rock song plays. Tami stands still for a moment, then lets the beat start to move her until she is finally doing her own "tension-release happy dance." The music should have a section that moves into a louder or more "rocking" section, and when that section hits, the lights should shift abruptly to "rock concert stadium lighting," with Tami grabbing a marker from the desk as a microphone and lip-synching the song. Her cell phone rings, and the lights click back to normal as she stops abruptly. With a wary look at the phone, she shuts off the music and picks it up.)*
TAMI. *(Slowly, afraid.)* Hello? *(It's not the bus with an emergency, so she relaxes a bit.)* Oh, hi, Amanda. *(Pause.)* Oh. *(Disappointed.)* Yeah, I know, it is scary. *(Pause.)* Sure, I understand. *(Bill enters, turning up the sleeves of his shirt.)* Any chance he might still come this weekend, since there isn't time to … *(Pause. Bill stops what he's doing because he realizes what the phone conversation is about.)* Okay. So do you have some new staff getting trained to work with Josh?

(Pause.) Yeah. *(Pause.)* OK. I know you are. Thanks. Bye. *(Bill gives her a quizzical look.)* Amanda. *(Bill doesn't remember who that is.)* The staffing coordinator at …
BILL. I thought it was Julie.
TAMI. She left.
BILL. Right, you told me …
TAMI. Justin won't be coming back to work with Josh. Not after last weekend. *(A beat.)* Why do you say you're okay working with a kid who might be aggressive and then quit when the kid is aggressive? *(Bill shrugs.)* And of course they don't have anyone else available right now. And even if they did, we'd need to get Matt in here to train them on Josh's behavior plan. So this weekend is shot.
BILL. Well, is it time for us push harder on the group home thing?
TAMI. What do you mean?
BILL. We can't seem to get reliable staff here. I assume the group homes have better luck.
TAMI. There isn't a good place available right now.
BILL. But we could get him on a waiting list.
TAMI. There's waiting lists for the waiting lists — and that's not gonna take care of this weekend. Can you take your mom out to the mall or something on Saturday morning?
BILL. Sure.
TAMI. I'll get someone to show that house for me so I can be here with Josh in the morning, and then I'll take him swimming in the afternoon so you guys can be back here. Then he should be tired out and mellow.
BILL. Okay. *(Tami crosses toward the kitchen.)* Should we get Mom a room at the Country Inn?
TAMI. She said she didn't want that, right? You told her about him and she still wanted to be here.
BILL. Yeah, I told her, but you know … Hearing isn't the same as …
TAMI. Just be sure she knows the code words, and let her know the hotel thing is still an option if things get crazy here. Oh — and Sunday … she can go to church with you, and I'll stay here with Josh.
BILL. Or I could stay here, and you could go to church with her.
TAMI. She's your mom.
BILL. Alright. And we'll figure out something for the afternoon. *(Tami rubs her forehead or some gesture of frustration.)* You okay?

TAMI. Sure. Just figuring things out.
BILL. Neck rub?
TAMI. Tempting!
BILL. I took the whole day off — there's time. *(He gestures toward the couch. Tami puts on a jacket or sweater as she talks.)*
TAMI. Groceries, flyers, office, paperwork for summer school … And you took the day off so you could finish getting the guest room ready, remember?
BILL. True.
TAMI. Will you hang up that calendar she sent us?
BILL. *(Laughing.)* Oh, yes. So … how many minutes do you think?
TAMI. What?
BILL. Once she's here, how many minutes till she pulls out the Bible? Let's make a bet.
TAMI. Be nice.
BILL. Hey, she's my mom.
TAMI. Still … .
BILL. It'll be before dinner, you know it.
TAMI. Well, whenever any problem presents itself.
BILL. That could be the second she opens the door!
TAMI. She means well. I wish it was that easy for me.
BILL. No bet?
TAMI. Alright. Five minutes.
BILL. I think … I'll go with fifteen.
TAMI. And the winner gets…?
BILL. Well, you know what I'd pick.
TAMI. And the winner gets … to sleep in for a week!
BILL. Okay.
TAMI. Okay. *(They nod and move simultaneously out of the room. Blackout. Tami's "rock star" music plays during the transition.)*

Scene Two

Around 3:00 that same afternoon. Bill and Grammy enter. Bill is carrying two suitcases. Grammy is walking with a 4-legged metal cane and carries a large purse.

BILL. *(Calling out.)* Hello?
TAMI. *(Offstage.)* I'll be out in a second.
BILL. *(He drops the mail on the table near the door.)* Mom, have a seat, I'll put these in the guest room for you. *(Grammy sits on the couch; Bill exits as Tami steps in from the kitchen and crosses to greet Grammy. Tami has a glass of tea that she is sipping.)*
TAMI. Hey there, *(Sees the cane.)* — Whoa, what happened?
GRAMMY. Oh, I was getting some of Clyde's books ready to put in storage and accidentally kicked one of the boxes — broke two toes.
TAMI. Oh, no! I'm sorry.
GRAMMY. Ah, it was my own fault — I just wasn't paying attention.
TAMI. Does it hurt?
GRAMMY. Not so much today. 'Course I have some pills that help that. *(She pats her bag. Bill enters.)*
BILL. Okay, Mom, your stuff's in the room.
TAMI. *(To Bill.)* Just made some iced tea.
BILL. Great. *(As he crosses.)* Mom?
GRAMMY. Sure. With two packets of the pink stuff please.
BILL. *(Stopping.)* I don't think we have any of that. *(He looks to Tami.)*
TAMI. Sorry — just regular sugar. Or honey?
GRAMMY. *(Reaching into her purse and pulling out a plastic baggy full of pink sugar substitute packets.)* That's OK — I always bring some with me. *(Bill nods and exits to the kitchen for the tea. Grammy pulls out two packets, then puts the baggy back in her purse. Tami sits.)*
TAMI. So, um. Josh will be home soon, and I wanted to make sure you were ready.
GRAMMY. Oh, yes! *(Reaching into her purse again.)* I have his present right here! *(She pulls out a brightly wrapped present.)*
TAMI. Great! Did Bill tell you about how he gets upset sometimes?

GRAMMY. And something about peanut butter and jelly? I'm not sure I got that right. *(Bill enters with two glasses of tea.)*
TAMI. It's a code we have to let each other know …
GRAMMY. Yeah, he said that. I don't quite … *(Bill hands her a glass of tea.)* Oh, thanks, Bill. *(Bill takes the other glass of tea with him as he crosses down by the door to flip through the day's mail.)* Spoon? *(Bill looks up from mail.)*
TAMI. It's okay, I'll get it.
BILL. Oh, I'm sorry, I'll … *(Tami exits to the kitchen. Bill puts down the mail and looks out the front door. An explanation.)* Bus should be here soon.
GRAMMY. When does Lisa get home?
BILL. Not sure today. Tami?
TAMI. *(Entering with spoon that she gives to Grammy.)* Yeah?
BILL. Lisa? When's she home today?
TAMI. She's doing supper at Lori's. Probably around seven?
GRAMMY. I'm so glad it worked out for me to get here.
TAMI. Yeah, so they're fixing all the plumbing this week, and then…?
GRAMMY. It's supposed to go up for sale once that's done … I'm just going to keep boxing things up …
BILL. Too bad they had to rip all the plumbing out.
GRAMMY. But this way I get to visit you. All things work together for good! *(Grammy reaches in her purse — Bill and Tami watch expectantly — Grammy pulls out the packet of pink sugar substitute and puts her "empties" in it. Bill and Tami react.)*
TAMI. Anyway, about Josh. I just want you to know that he's probably not going to be a problem, but if he is …
GRAMMY. I can't wait to see him! When Clyde got so sick and we couldn't travel, I missed — what — three Christmases?
BILL. *(Going out the door.)* Bus is here.
TAMI. *(Going to stand by door.)* He has some things he always does right when he gets home — takes off his vest, puts away his lunchbox and backpack.
GRAMMY. Okay.
TAMI. I don't want you to feel like he's ignoring you.
GRAMMY. I remember how he is. *(Grammy stands and picks up present as Josh and Bill come through door. They close the door and Josh stands still while Bill unzips his vest. Josh takes off the vest as Tami takes the bookbag and grabs a notebook out of it. Josh takes the vest and his*

bookbag out to the kitchen, making happy sounds as he goes. Grammy holds out the present while all this is happening, but Josh ignores her.)
TAMI. *(Reading from the book.)* Good day. They went shopping and cooked pizzas. Josh liked making them but didn't eat them.
BILL. No surprise there. *(Josh comes back in carrying a large jar containing marbles, which he gives to Tami.)*
TAMI. That's right — you had safe hands today! Good job! *(She opens the jar and Josh squeals with excitement. He ponders for a short second, grabs a marble and runs out to his room.)*
BILL. *(To Grammy.)* You remember that big marble run he has? *(Tami takes the notebook and the marble jar out to the kitchen.)*
GRAMMY. Yes.
BILL. When he has a good day at school, he gets to pick a new marble.
GRAMMY. He sure has grown — my goodness!
BILL. Yes, hopefully he's done now. *(Moving toward hallway, calling out.)* Josh — come on out and see who's here. *(Josh enters.)* Grammy Sue is here — look!
GRAMMY. Josh — come here and give Grammy a hug! I have a present for you. *(Josh comes to her and allows her to hug him, then rips the paper off the box. He examines it closely for a few seconds, then drops it on the floor and runs to the computer. Tami comes back in as Josh sits and plays at the computer.)*
TAMI. Oh, let me see — what is it?
GRAMMY. It's a puzzle with a train. He still likes puzzles, doesn't he?
BILL. I'm sure he'll want to help later on. *(He takes the puzzle box and gets a puzzle board out from behind the bookcase, speaking to Josh as he moves.)* Josh — we're going to start the puzzle Grammy brought you. You can come help when you're ready. *(Bill puts the board on the dining room table and opens the box.)*
GRAMMY. So, how are things at your church? *(Tami looks at Bill, who dumps the puzzle pieces on the table and begins sorting them.)*
TAMI. Fine, I think. We haven't gotten there in a while.
GRAMMY. You know our prayer group lifts up Josh every week.
TAMI. *(Genuinely.)* That's great. Thanks.
GRAMMY. We have such a nice program for the disabled kids — I wish your church had one.
TAMI. It mostly works out best if one of us stays home with him.
GRAMMY. But he's a part of the church family, he should be there.

TAMI. *(Crossing to the table to help with the puzzle.)* You know, sometimes there are distant relatives in a family that you don't get to see very often.

GRAMMY. Yes, well ... *(She remembers something and reaches in her purse to pull out her Bible. Tami and Bill look at his watch and Tami does a victory dance. Bill pouts momentarily.)* There's a verse in here that I want to share with you. Here it is: "For I know the plans I have for you," declares the Lord, "plans to prosper you and not to harm you, plans to give you hope and a future." *Jeremiah* 29:11. That verse was on my heart for your family.

TAMI. Thank you. *(Josh picks up a toy and heads toward the door to put it with other toys near there.)*

GRAMMY. Josh is here for a reason. God has a plan.

TAMI. We know that. *(Grammy reaches for her cane but accidentally knocks it over. Josh turns at the noise and sees the cane, which looks like medical equipment to him and scares him. He does his head-to-forehead stress gesture, which Bill sees.)*

BILL. It's okay — Grammy hurt her foot, and so she's using this to help her walk. *(To Grammy.)* Can I show this to him? *(She nods. He puts it on the floor, not too near Josh.)* This is called a cane. *(Teaching mode.)* What's it called?

JOSH. Cane.

BILL. Good, that's right. You can touch it.

JOSH. No touch it.

BILL. No problem buddy. I just wanted you to see what it was. It helps Grammy walk. She needs it. *(Josh has crossed down to the table in part to get away from the cane and in part to see the picture on the front of the puzzle box. He takes the box cover and walks across the room with it.)*

GRAMMY. We're going to need that picture to figure out how to put this together, Joshy. Can you bring it back to Grammy? *(Josh brings the box back, then reaches and grabs both hands full of puzzle pieces, which he throws in the air. As they fall down, he shrieks and does his happy dance. Surprised.)* Joshy!

TAMI. Wow — Okay — that was fun! *(She pauses to let Josh finish his happy dance.)* Now come and help us pick up the pieces. *(Josh comes over and helps pick them up. Bill also helps. A buzzer sounds from the kitchen. Josh reacts to the sound.)* It's OK, Josh. Mom is cooking a pie — I'll be back in a sec. *(Tami exits to kitchen. Josh sits on the floor and turns on the TV. Bill continues picking up pieces,*

and Grammy sorts. Josh makes the video go super-fast and we hear the dialogue speed up to "chipmunk" mode.)
GRAMMY. Bill, could I get just a little more tea?
BILL. Oh, sure. *(He gets her glass and takes it out into the kitchen. Josh squeals and Grammy moves to see what he's watching. He pulls up his shirt and touches both nipples throughout Grammy's next speech.)*
GRAMMY. Joshy, that's not nice. It's not polite to touch your chest like that. *(Josh continues as before. She speaks louder.)* Josh! *(Bill enters with the glass of tea. He sees Josh.)*
BILL. Josh — shirt down. *(Josh pulls his shirt down.)* Clap hands. *(Josh does.)* Good job! *(Josh turns his focus back on the TV and turns down the volume. Bill puts the iced tea down in front of Grammy and sits down to sort through puzzle pieces. Once Bill is absorbed in the puzzle pieces, Josh puts his hands down his pants.)*
GRAMMY. You need to teach him to listen to other people.
BILL. What?
GRAMMY. I told him it wasn't polite to have his shirt up like that, and he just ignored me.
BILL. I'm sorry. He doesn't really get a concept like being polite. *(Grammy glances over to Josh and sees what he is doing. She turns her head away with a sharp intake of breath. Bill looks over at Josh.)* Josh, look at me. *(Josh does.)* Do you need to go to your room?
JOSH. No room.
BILL. Then hands up.
JOSH. No hands up.
BILL. Then you need to go to your room to be private.
JOSH. No private.
BILL. Do you want feathers? Let's show Grandma feathers. *(Josh considers this for a moment then runs up under the feather box, does his ritual and releases the feathers.)*
GRAMMY. That looks like fun. *(As Josh finishes his happy dance, Grammy crosses to the couch and gets two more "pink packets" out of her purse and also a bottle of pills. She takes them back to the table. She stirs the pink stuff into her tea and then swallows her pills. She sets the pillbox on the table. Bill and Josh retrieve the feathers as the conversation continues.)*
GRAMMY. He understands "private"?
BILL. Well, not exactly — he just knows that if he wants to do — that behavior — he needs to be in his room. And maybe he connects it with "private parts" which is how we talk about his — you know.

GRAMMY. Ah. Yes. Well. *(She crosses back to work the puzzle as Tami enters from kitchen. Josh leans on wall and puts his hands down his pants.)*
TAMI. Pie smells good, doesn't it.
BILL. Yeah, I think we might need to sample it now to make sure it's okay. *(Seeing Josh.)* Josh. *(Josh looks at him.)* Hands up or go to your room. *(A beat, and Josh exits with happy noises.)*
TAMI. *(A little laugh.)* Time for some privacy! *(Back to the previous conversation, not fazed by Josh's activity.)* So — you want some pie now?
BILL. No, I was kidding — but — Mom ... pie now?
GRAMMY. *(Still recovering from the Josh incident.)* I'll wait. Thanks.
TAMI. *(Putting a piece in place. She laughs, remembering.)* At least he didn't he take the drugstore flyer in with him this time.
GRAMMY. Drugstore flyer?
TAMI. Yeah. Well, he kinda likes to look at the diaper ads.
GRAMMY. The diaper ads?
BILL. It's nothing, really.
TAMI. Ever since he was potty trained, for some reason, he's really enjoyed the feeling of plastic, like a diaper, on his skin, so when ...
BILL. It's a sensory thing. You remember that "sensory diet" we ...
TAMI. So, a few weeks ago I was in his room and found this stash of drugstore ads, you know the ones that come in the Sunday paper? And I couldn't figure out why he would have them there, and then I saw they were all turned to the section where there were sales on diapers.
BILL. Hey — look — we've got all four corner pieces now. Anybody seen a match for this one?
GRAMMY. So he likes to look at diaper ads?
TAMI. Yeah. We call it Joshy porn.
BILL. Did you...?
TAMI. What? It's funny.
GRAMMY. It's not ...
TAMI. What?
GRAMMY. I mean, isn't that, you know, um — worrisome?
TAMI. Why? I mean — he's not going to attack some child or ...
GRAMMY. Well, I didn't think he would do that, it's ...
TAMI. He's scared of the sound of babies crying so he won't even go near them.
GRAMMY. It just seems ...

BILL. ... like too much information? I agree!

GRAMMY. No, it seems, unnatural.

TAMI. What should we do, show him pictures of women in bikinis and teach him to masturbate while looking at them?

BILL. Okay! *(Standing.)* I'm going to go get the puzzle glue in the basement. *(He exits. Tami and Grammy sort puzzle pieces in silence. Grammy is trying to figure out what to say.)*

TAMI. I'm sorry. I shouldn't talk about this stuff.

GRAMMY. I'm just, um — I don't really know what to say.

TAMI. It's okay. Most of the time I don't either.

GRAMMY. It seems wrong, somehow.

TAMI. We have to laugh about stuff. Or else we'll get stuck.

GRAMMY. It is good to see you laugh. *(Tami smiles. A beat.)* Whenever we talk on the phone, you seem so worried, so distracted.

TAMI. It can be a little crazy here, you know.

GRAMMY. I feel like, well ...

TAMI. What?

GRAMMY. Like you're not really trusting God.

TAMI. And what would that look like?

GRAMMY. You'd be more at peace. Less worried.

TAMI. Well, I'm trusting God as much as I can.

GRAMMY. But that's just it. There's no conditions on God's love for us, so we shouldn't put conditions on our love for him.

TAMI. *(A sigh.)* I appreciate that you want us to be at peace with our situation.

GRAMMY. It's more than ...

TAMI. I would say that my relationship with God isn't conditional, it's just complicated. *(Josh enters with a DVD in one hand and his fist to his forehead, already agitated.)*

JOSH. Fix it. Fix it. DVD fix it.

TAMI. *(Standing and crossing to him.)* OK, let me see. Probably it just needs to be cleaned.

JOSH. Fix it DVD.

TAMI. Uh oh, Josh — look here at this crack on the DVD. I think it's broken. *(Trying to lighten the situation, with a silly voice.)* Uh oh, time for a new DVD!

JOSH. *(Both fists to forehead, loudly.)* No new!

TAMI. Let's go back in your room and find a different DVD to watch.

JOSH. *(Louder.)* No room! Fix it DVD!

TAMI. This DVD is broken, but you could watch another DVD, or you can play on the computer, or we could do feathers. Let me write it down for you. *(As Tami moves to get paper and pen she speaks quietly to Grammy.)* Grammy, it might be time for you to get some … *(Before she can finish, Josh screams and lunges at her, grabbing her hair with one hand while biting on the other hand.)* You need to relax, Josh. Show me relax. *(Josh bites his hand harder, shaking with frustration. Grammy stands as if to come and help and Tami waves her off until she sits back down. Tami works at staying calm, even though the hair-pulling is painful.)* Sip in a breath, come on, sip it in with me. *(She "sips" in a breath four times.)* Now blow it out with me. *(She blows out four times.)* Come on Josh. Sip in. *(She sips in and Josh starts to join her, still holding onto her hair, but relaxing the hand that he is biting.)* Good, now blow it out. *(She blows out four times and Josh does it with her.)* Sip in. *(They do.)* And blow out. *(They do.)* Good! Now show me relax. *(Josh lets go of her hair and folds his hands together.)* Good job! Let's do ten "relax." *(She folds her hands the same way and they count together, bobbing their hands up and down as they do.)* One, two, three, four, five, six, seven, eight, nine, ten. Great relaxing Josh! Now let me write your three choices. *(She gets the paper and pen and writes as she talks.)* Here are your choices right now. One: Watch DVD. Two: Play computer. Three: Do feathers. *(She puts the pen in his hand.)* Circle which choice you want right now. *(Josh frowns and pushes pen back in her hand.)* Circle which choice you want right now: *(She puts pen in his hand and points at each number as she says them.)* one, two or three. *(Josh frowns, but circles #1.)* Good job choosing! You chose number one — watch another DVD in your room! Do you need some help?
JOSH. No help. *(He exits to his room.)*
GRAMMY. *(Standing.)* Are you okay?
TAMI. He should be fine now — I need to grab something from the kitchen — I'll be right back. *(She exits. Grammy crosses to couch, putting her pills on the lower shelf of the coffee table as she grabs her Bible. Tami enters holding something on her head and carrying a glass of wine.)*
GRAMMY. What is that?
TAMI. This *(Gesturing to wine glass.)* is Shiraz, and this *(Gesture to her head.)* is a package of frozen organic blueberries. Have some? *(Grammy doesn't know what to say. Lights down. Tami exits.)*

Scene Three

An hour or so later. Lights up — Grammy is trying to move the puzzle board to the coffee table. Tami enters with plates, napkins and silverware for setting the table.

TAMI. Don't worry — I'll get that.
GRAMMY. I can — let me help.
TAMI. Well, here, you set the table and I'll move the puzzle. *(Tami moves the puzzle as we hear barking outside the front door. Lisa enters, excited.)*
LISA. Mom, the cutest dog is outside.
TAMI. What?
LISA. Oh, Grammy! *(She moves to give her a hug, then sees the cane.)* What happened?
GRAMMY. Broke two toes!
LISA. Ouch! Sorry for the toes. *(She hugs Grammy, then turns to Tami.)* Mom …
TAMI. I thought you were at Lori's for supper.
LISA. Her Mom gave me a ride home 'cuz Lori didn't feel good. And this dog was just waiting! *(Tami crosses up to look out the front door.)*
TAMI. It probably belongs to someone around here. If it's still here after supper, you can get some rope from the garage and walk it around the neighborhood.
LISA. *(Collapsing on the couch.)* But I've never seen him and I walk around all the time.
TAMI. Having a dog is complicated.
LISA. But … .
TAMI. We're not going to decide this right now.
LISA. *(Moving to her Mom.)* But he's sooooo cute! *(Tami smiles. The dog starts barking again.)*
TAMI. I know. Can you go get some glasses and water for us for supper?
LISA. Okay. *(Lisa exits. Tami finishes moving the puzzle, and Grammy finishes setting the table. Josh enters from his room.)*
JOSH. Barking.

TAMI. Yes, there is a dog barking.
JOSH. No barking.
TAMI. You don't like the dog barking.
JOSH. You don't … *(Tami interrupts him with sign language prompting the word "I.")* I don't like dog barking. *(He pushes his fist to his forehead.)*
TAMI. That's really good telling me how you feel, Josh. We'll help the dog stop barking, okay? Lisa?! *(Lisa comes in with a couple of glasses of water.)*
LISA. Yeah?
TAMI. Can you put the dog in the garage while we eat supper?
LISA. Why?
JOSH. No barking! *(Lisa rolls her eyes and walks to the front door. She slams the door and takes the dog away. The barking fades.)*
TAMI. Lisa is helping the dog. Listen. Barking is all done.
JOSH. Dog is barking
TAMI. No more barking. Dog is gone. *(Josh has spied the pill bottle on the table. He picks it up and shakes it, listening to the noise.)*
GRAMMY. Those are mine, Josh. Bring the pills to Grammy. *(Josh keeps shaking the pills.)*
TAMI. *(Holding out her hand.)* No pills for Josh. Pills for Grammy. Are you dancing? Are you dancing? *(Josh continues shaking the bottle. He does rhythmic movement while shaking the pills. Tami watches him and then joins in with his movement. They laugh together.)*
TAMI. *(Holding out her hand.)* Mommy's turn. Nice dancing, Josh. *(Josh hands her the pills, and she shakes them and they move again.)* Now Grammy's turn. *(She takes the pills to Grammy. Josh waits for her to shake them.)*
GRAMMY. Umm? *(She looks to Tami.)*
TAMI. *(Urgently.)* Grammy's turn to shake the pills. *(Grammy hesitantly shakes the pills, and Josh moves again. Applauding.)* Nice dancing! Josh, it's time for supper. Do you want to eat with us?
JOSH. No supper! *(He exits back to his room. We hear a children's music video playing loudly, then his door closes.)*
GRAMMY. No supper?
TAMI. He likes to eat by himself.
GRAMMY. Oh. I thought we would all …
TAMI. Or I should say, he doesn't like to watch other people eat. It grosses him out.
GRAMMY. So you don't eat together, as a family?

TAMI. We do. Lisa and Bill and I, and you — we'll eat together as a family.
GRAMMY. Well, yes, but I meant …
TAMI. And Josh will be happy NOT eating with us, and if Josh is happy, then we'll all be happy! *(Lisa enters through the kitchen.)*
LISA. Dog in garage by order of his Highness.
TAMI. Thank you. Did you latch the back door? *(Lisa nods and Tami exits to the kitchen.)*
GRAMMY. What kind of dog is it?
LISA. *(Crossing to her.)* It looks kinda like a Lab. A chocolate Lab, but smaller.
GRAMMY. Labs are good dogs.
LISA. I won't get to keep it.
GRAMMY. I don't know, your Mom seemed like …
LISA. Josh said "no barking." So no dog.
GRAMMY. Well, I'm sure he could get used to it.
LISA. I wish.
GRAMMY. Wait and see.
LISA. Right. It probably belongs to someone already anyway.
GRAMMY. I wanted to get a dog after your Dad went to college, but Grandpa thought it'd be too much work. But now that he's in heaven, I think it might be a good idea!
LISA. I thought you were selling the house?
GRAMMY. Sure, I'm going to get a smaller place, but there'll be room for a dog. Then when you and your dad come to visit next summer …
LISA. My Josh-free vacation.
GRAMMY. Your dad had a collie when he was seven or eight, I think. He called it …
LISA. Maybe I should come and stay all summer.
GRAMMY. Oh?
LISA. I could actually have people over. I could have a barking dog. There wouldn't be *(She kicks the coffee table so the pieces fall on the floor.)* stupid puzzle pieces all over the place.
GRAMMY. Well, sweetie, of course, if you …
LISA. Or maybe Josh could go away for a long vacation and never come back.
GRAMMY. Lisa!
LISA. I wish. *(She moves to the table, setting silverware and napkins out.)*
GRAMMY. I'm sure your parents wouldn't want you to talk like that.

LISA. I know.

GRAMMY. I know Josh is a challenge.

LISA. You don't know.

GRAMMY. I know you're a big help for your mom. And I'm sure that Josh, well, he does what he can, to be, helpful.

LISA. *(Sarcastic.)* Right. Helpful giving bruises, breaking her finger.

GRAMMY. Oh. How often does he get upset like that?

LISA. I don't know. It depends. Sometimes he's good for months and sometimes it's every other day.

GRAMMY. Has he — gotten upset — with you?

LISA. *(Turning away.)* I mostly just keep away from him now.

GRAMMY. *(Moving toward her.)* Oh, honey, I'm sorry.

LISA. *(Returning to her table activity.)* Whatever. *(From the kitchen we hear Tami call.)*

TAMI. Bill, supper. *(Tami enters with a glass of water and her glass of wine, which she sets at the table.)*

TAMI. Lisa?

LISA. Yeah?

TAMI. Can you help Dad bring in the food?

LISA. Sure. *(She exits as Grammy moves to the dining room table. Tami sees the puzzle pieces on the floor and moves to pick them up. Josh enters and starts pacing back and forth upstage, moving between his happy dance and repeating a few lines of dialogue from a Tarzan movie or* George of the Jungle. *Lisa and Bill enter with food. Tami joins them at the table, and they all sit.)*

TAMI. *(To Grammy.)* Would you like to say the blessing?

GRAMMY. Yes. *(They bow their heads. Josh is still scripting.)* Dearest Lord, we thank you for each and every blessing here in this room today, and for the wonderful food you have provided for us. *(Josh does a "Tarzan" yell and the crash noise. Grammy looks up, then works to incorporate the noise into her prayer.)* And ... and for all the ways in which we praise you. Amen.

TAMI and BILL. Amen. *(A beat as they all start to eat and Josh finds a scene to watch on the computer.)*

GRAMMY. Bill, I was trying to remember, what was the name of that dog you had?

BILL. Oh. Hmmm. *(Remembering.)* Heidi!

GRAMMY. It was a girl dog? I don't remember that.

BILL. I assume it was a girl, since I named it Heidi.

LISA. You named a dog Heidi?

BILL. I have no idea why.
GRAMMY. *(To Lisa.)* Did I ever show you that picture of him in his Boy Scout's uniform and the dog has on a kerchief matching his?
LISA. I don't remember that. *(They eat as Josh paces and repeats phrases from the scene he's watching on his computer, which is a cartoon involving rocks and rollercoasters and trains. Grammy is distracted by him.)*
BILL. Food OK, Mom?
GRAMMY. Yes?
BILL. Is the food OK ... What you're eating?
GRAMMY. Oh, yes. Very good.
JOSH. Mom, help me.
TAMI. *(From the table.)* What do you need?
JOSH. Pushing on the rock.
TAMI. *(This is part of a script — in an animated voice.)* Oh my! What will happen?
JOSH. Look out!
TAMI. Is it falling?
JOSH. Mom, help me. *(Tami takes her wine glass and moves to Josh at the computer. She continues the conversation with Josh at a lower volume level, but can still be heard. Bill and Lisa are able to tune this out — Grammy is not.)*
TAMI. What's happening?

BILL. It's going to be weird to visit you and be in a different house!	JOSH. Look out!
GRAMMY. You know, I just couldn't keep up with all that space ...	TAMI. Oh no, what will they do?
BILL. I know. A smaller place makes sense, it's just ... Mom?	JOSH. Pushing on the rock.
GRAMMY. Yes? Oh, right ...	TAMI. They're pushing.
LISA. Where are you looking?	JOSH. Stucking.
GRAMMY. Umm, I'm not sure — I saw one place by the docks.	TAMI. It IS stuck. Yikes!
LISA. Closer to the mini golf.	JOSH. Falling!
BILL. That would be nice.	TAMI. Oh no! Look out!
GRAMMY. Oh, yes. Right.	JOSH. *(Laughing.)* Crashing!

(The dog barking is heard again, soft and growing louder.)

TAMI. *(Continuing the script.)* Oh dear! How do they feel?
JOSH. *(Distracted.)* Barking.
TAMI. *(To Lisa.)* Sounds like it got out of the garage. Did you close the door all the way?
LISA. There's that hole near the street side — I didn't think he could fit through. *(The barking continues, sounding like it's near the kitchen side of the house.)*
JOSH. *(Stands, a frown.)* Barking.
BILL. It's alright, buddy, the dog is just saying "Hello."
JOSH. Hello, dog.
BILL. That's right. Hello dog.
JOSH. Hello, dog. No barking.
BILL. Barking is okay. He's just saying hello.
JOSH. Hello, Barking No.
TAMI. Josh, why don't you go read a book in your room, and we'll take care of the barking dog.
JOSH. No barking dog.
TAMI. I know you don't like the sound of the barking dog.
JOSH. No barking dog.
LISA. *(Throwing her napkin onto her plate and picking it up.)* Who needs to eat? *(Lisa exits to the kitchen. Bill stands and looks at Tami.)*
BILL. I'll help her? *(Tami nods. Bill takes his plate to the kitchen [will exit through the back door to help catch the dog]. Tami stands.)*
TAMI. Josh, let's go to your room and see where Cookie Monster is. *(The barking continues, and Josh starts to bite his hand and shake in frustration. For every bark, Josh gives a corresponding little scream or groan, as if the sounds are hitting him physically. To Grammy.)* Ummm ... It looks like we could use some "peanut butter" in here ... why don't you go into the kitchen for that?
GRAMMY. Oh. Well. Yes. *(Grammy exits, and Tami continues trying to soothe/distract Josh. The dog barking gets louder, and we hear Lisa and Bill shouting as they try to catch the dog, which has run around to near the front door again.)*
JOSH. Barking! Barking! Barking!
TAMI. I know! It is loud! Let's cover our ears. *(She covers her ears and tries to get him to cover his. The barking continues. Josh is finally at his breaking point, and with a scream he lunges for Tami, one hand pressing on his forehead and the other grabbing her shirt near the neck. He pulls her close to him and screams again, then slams her against the door, his hands around her throat. Tami is working to pry his hands from her*

as she tries to talk calmly.) Let's breathe. *(She takes a deep breath in and blows in and out.)* Come on, sip a breath in *(She sips like on a straw, and Josh does as well.)* and blow it out. *(They both blow. Josh is beginning to relax, although he still has a grip on her shirt.)* Sip it in *(They do.)* and blow it out. *(Grammy pushes the door open with her cane, which makes a loud noise, and enters carrying two jars of peanut butter.)*

GRAMMY. I didn't know if you wanted creamy or crunchy … *(She accidentally drops one or both of them.)* Oh dear! *(Josh lets go of Tami and lunges toward Grammy.)*

TAMI. JELLY! JELLY! *(Josh has Grammy by the shirt now, and she is using her cane to try and push him away. Tami somehow squeezes herself underneath Josh's arm and in between Josh and Grammy, getting right into Josh's face.)* Let go of Grammy. Let go of Grammy. Josh, look at me. *(Josh grabs Tami's shirt with both hands and lets go of Grammy, who falls to the floor. The front door opens and Lisa runs in laughing.)*

LISA. Dad finally caught him and … *(She stops abruptly as she takes in the scene. Tami sees Lisa and moves herself between Josh and Lisa and pushes him upstage as much as she can.)*

TAMI. *(To Lisa.)* Take Grammy to her room. *(Lisa helps Grammy up, and they exit as Josh screams and Tami continues speaking quietly to him.)* Josh — look at Mommy. The barking is stopped. The barking is gone.

JOSH. *(Screaming.)* Barking! Barking! *(Bill runs in from the kitchen and sees the situation. He moves behind Josh and does a "bear hug" around him, forcing Josh's arms down by his sides. Josh is still holding Tami by the shirt with both hands. Tami slithers out of her shirt, which Josh continues to hold. In her bra and pants, she backs away slowly toward the kitchen door. Josh looks at the shirt, takes a big breath, and begins crying a plaintive, sad howl. All the energy drains from him and he slides to the floor, continuing his cry.)* I'm sorry. *(This signals the end of an "episode." Bill slowly loosens his grip on Josh, who crumples to the ground, continuing to howl and cry and say "I'm sorry." Bill moves toward Tami, who points toward the hallway.)*

TAMI. Go check on your mom and Lisa.

BILL. Did he…?

TAMI. Your mom. Lisa took her out. *(Bill exits quickly as Tami warily moves toward Josh.)*

JOSH. Mom I'm sorry Mom I'm sorry.

TAMI. Can I have my shirt back? *(Josh holds out the shirt and Tami grabs it and puts it back on, noting where/how it's stretched out.)*

JOSH. *(Sobbing.)* Mom I'm sorry Mom I'm sorry.
TAMI. *(Holding back tears.)* I know you're sorry, Joshy, I just wish … *(The tears come.)* you could be sorry before you grabbed. I wish you … *(Tami moves to the hutch, grabbing two glasses.)*
JOSH. *(Sadly.)* Mom is crying.
TAMI. Yes, Mom is crying. *(Tami pulls a bottle of whiskey from the cabinet under the hutch as Bill enters. She pours two shots and drinks hers.)*
JOSH. Mom is sad.
BILL. She's okay — feels bad about forgetting about the peanut butter thing.
TAMI. *(Holding the glass out to Bill.)* Have one? *(Bill nods "no" and sits next to Josh on the couch. Tami drinks the shot, puts the bottle away and takes the glasses out to the kitchen.)*
BILL. You okay now, buddy? *(No response from Josh, who is now putting one hand over his left eye, then removing it, then repeating.)* Do you want a drink of water? *(Josh switches to hand over his right eye, comparing the results.)* Josh. Josh. Look at Dad. *(Josh looks at him.)* Do you want some water?
JOSH. Water.
BILL. Water yes or water no?
JOSH. Water yes.
BILL. How about if you go read some books, and I'll bring you a glass of water.
JOSH. Pockorn.
BILL. You want popcorn? *(Tami enters and watches Bill and Josh.)*
JOSH. Pockorn. Yes.
BILL. Okay. I'll pop some popcorn, and you go read books in your room. *(Josh smiles and begins to make happy sounds again and exits to his room. Bill watches to be sure Josh is in his room, then moves toward the kitchen. There's nothing else to say.)* Pockorn. Want some?
TAMI. *(Trying to smile.)* No, thanks. *(He touches Tami on the shoulder for a moment before he exits to the kitchen. Lisa enters and sits on the couch. There is a long silence.)*
LISA. Grammy wants me to come live with her.
TAMI. Oh. *(Pause.)* Do you want to?
LISA. Do you want me to? *(Tami sighs and rubs her forehead.)* Well?
TAMI. I want you to live here, but if you want to go live with Grammy, I would understand. *(Lisa reaches forward and pulls pieces of the puzzle apart.)* You know we're trying to find a place for Josh to live.
LISA. Just lock him up.

TAMI. *(This is a conversation they've had too many times before.)* Really? We have to talk again about why he doesn't need hospitaliza*(tion)* …
LISA. *(Interrupting.)* I was calling the police, and Grammy made me put down the phone.
TAMI. Do we…? Look. I know you're scared, and I'm …
LISA. I'm not scared for me. I'll just get a knife and …
TAMI. Lisa.
LISA. I should have just …
TAMI. Stop.
LISA. He could have killed Grammy.
TAMI. But he didn't.
LISA. He could have.
TAMI. But he …
LISA. It only takes one time to be dead. One time.
TAMI. *(A beat.)* He's not going to …
LISA. You don't know that. You don't know what he will do.
TAMI. He's not going to …
LISA. He's a freak and he should be locked up!
TAMI. If there was a safe place for him to live, don't you think we would have moved him there?
LISA. You keep saying that, but I don't know if you'd think any place was good enough for your precious baby boy.
TAMI. I really am trying to keep you safe. I know he's scary. And I know you hate him. And that's okay — you can hate him. But moms don't get that choice. *(Her voice cracks.)* We can't help it — we just love our kids, no matter what.
LISA. *(Fighting back her own tears.)* It's all just so stupid. Everything. I wish he would just go away forever.
TAMI. I know.
LISA. You don't know. If you did, you'd get him out of this house!
TAMI. We just went through this. We're working on it.
LISA. Well, work harder!
TAMI. Calm down.
LISA. Why should I? He gets to do whatever the hell he wants *(She knocks something down, a challenge, and looks at Tami.)*
TAMI. *(A pause, shifting gears.)* Do you want to help clear the table or set out dessert?
LISA. *(A pause.)* Don't treat me like him.
TAMI. Don't act like him.

LISA. Bitch.

TAMI. *(A beat.)* Do you want to help clear the table or set out dessert?

LISA. I want better choices. *(Bill enters with a large bowl of popcorn and a glass of water. He may notice the tension in the room, but decides not to address it. He exits to Josh's room.)*

TAMI. Don't we all.

LISA. Forget you. *(She exits to the kitchen.)* I hate this. I'd rather live with Grammy! *(Lisa exits. We hear children's music playing as he opens the door to Josh's room. The following offstage conversation takes place as Tami clears the table and Grammy enters. Tami exits with the dishes, and Grammy takes a few steps downstage.)*

BILL. *(Offstage.)* Here you go, buddy. Hey, I like your music! *(He starts singing along.)*

JOSH. *(Offstage.)* Dad. Stop singing.

BILL. *(Offstage.)* OK, buddy. What book are you reading?

JOSH. *(Offstage.)* Percy takes a plunge

BILL. *(Offstage.)* Here's your popcorn and water. Do you want Dad to come back later and read some books.

JOSH. *(Offstage.)* Later read some books. *(The children's music fades as Bill closes the door and comes back into the room.)*

BILL. I'm sorry, Mom.

GRAMMY. I didn't know. *(Tami takes more dishes out to the kitchen.)*

BILL. Know?

GRAMMY. It was like this. You said he got upset, I just didn't realize it was so … much.

BILL. Yeah, well — it probably looks worse to you. We're used to it. And — this — doesn't happen that much.

GRAMMY. There's no help? *(Tami enters and wipes off table.)*

TAMI. We have a hard time finding people who want to keep working with him. And, really, he's calmer when it's just us.

GRAMMY. But it won't always be just you. You can't expect Lisa to …

TAMI. *(Going back into the kitchen.)* We know.

BILL. We can get you a room at the Country Inn. If you want. It would be safer.

GRAMMY. Isn't there some medicine that would…? *(Tami comes back into the room.)*

BILL. He's taking three different things — if we up the dosages, he just gets more cranky.

GRAMMY. Isn't there a safe place that Josh could live? I thought now that he's 18 he could go to one of those group houses.
BILL. There's waiting lists.
TAMI. And they're not always "safe" places.
GRAMMY. There must be something.
TAMI. There is, we just haven't found it yet. We're working on it.
GRAMMY. We can ask God for the solution. *(Bill glances at Tami, who turns her head away.)* I know it's hard to trust. *(Holding out her hands to Bill and Tammy, an invitation.)* Can we have a prayer?
BILL. Ummm ...
GRAMMY. This is an awful situation. I can feel how your hearts are hurting. My heart is hurting. God's heart is hurting with us. Can we pray together?
TAMI. *(Quietly.)* For what?
GRAMMY. God can do anything. *(Bill turns away, fighting a response.)*
TAMI. Yes, but ...
GRAMMY. We can pray for healing. For a miracle: that Josh will be released from this autism.
TAMI. Because we've never done that since the minute he was diagnosed.
GRAMMY. We can pray with more power, together.
TAMI. And when nothing changes, again, then what?
GRAMMY. God is bigger than our doubts. *(She holds her hands out again to them.)*
BILL. Mom — if you're gonna pray, then ... *(Not too fast, with conviction.)* pray for programs and housing options and staff for people like Josh.
GRAMMY. Well, of course we can ...
BILL. Pray that — that Lisa won't hate us forever. Pray that our marriage won't fall apart. Pray that people will stop just praying and take some action.
GRAMMY. Healing is action. Why wouldn't you want him *[Healed]* ...
TAMI. It's not that we don't want him *[Healed.]* ...
BILL. *(Overriding them.)* God — said NO to that request a long time ago. *(A pause. Grammy stands.)*
GRAMMY. I'm going to take a rest.
BILL. Mom ... I'm ... *(Grammy keeps walking.)* There's still dessert.

GRAMMY. Maybe later. *(She turns to face them.)* You know, when you don't want to pray is the best time to do it. *(Grammy exits. Bill lets out a big breath, then looks to Tami.)*
BILL. Well, that's probably a good point.
TAMI. Yeah. Wanna pray?
BILL. Not sure God wants to hear what I have to say right now.
TAMI. Why's that?
BILL. Well, I just yelled at my crippled mother and basically gave Him the finger.
TAMI. Not really.
BILL. Got anything else you want me to screw up?
TAMI. You didn't screw up. She needed to hear that. You needed to say it.
BILL. Not screwing up should feel better than this.
TAMI. *(Sharply.)* I'm sorry.
BILL. *(Moving toward her.)* No, I'm sorry I was outside when — how badly did he get you?
TAMI. Not so bad. The shirt got the worst of it this time. *(Bill comes up behind her and encircles her in a hug, which she accepts. He brushes her hair away from her neck and leans down to kiss her neck. She pulls away.)*
BILL. OK. Sorry.
TAMI. It's not you.
BILL. Just trying to take your mind off …
TAMI. I know.
BILL. You keep pushing me away.
TAMI. I can't …
BILL. What?
TAMI. I can't take care of another person right now.
BILL. This is taking care of me?
TAMI. Isn't it?
BILL. I thought it was taking care of each other.
TAMI. I will fall apart if I let go. Why can't you…?
BILL. That's the whole point. You let go and relax!
TAMI. That's why wine was invented!
BILL. So … you'd rather have a glass of wine than let me touch you.
TAMI. You know what? Sex is your prayer for a miracle — *(Gesturing towards Josh's room.)* and look what that got us. *(Tami sits on the couch. Her words hang in the air.)*
BILL. *(A pause.)* I don't know what to say.
TAMI. Neither do I.

BILL. I'll go read a book with Josh. I think I'm still capable of that at least. *(Bill exits to bedroom and we hear the children's music again. Tami takes a deep breath, staring out in front of her. She brings her hands to her face [or some gesture of being overwhelmed]. The children's music abruptly cuts out and the lights shift to a cool blue on the room. Yelling offstage.)* Call 911. Call 911. He's not breathing. Call 911. *(Tami looks up, horrified. Lights fade as we hear sirens.)*

Scene Four

The following day. Lights in the room are cooler than before. Tami crosses up towards the front door, and then remembers she doesn't need to look for the bus. She crosses up to the computer and begins typing as Bill enters through the front door. Tami glances at him and then returns to her typing. Bill stands by the door until she stops typing and looks at him in earnest.

BILL. Done at the ... I mean, the arrangements are made. *(Tami nods.)* And your ... the — for the paper...? *(Tami shrugs and looks at the screen. Bill walks over and reads, almost resting his hand on her shoulder, but not quite.)* That's good. I like that you mention his marble collection. *(He walks toward the coffee table.)* Should I — the puzzle? *(Tami is back typing and doesn't hear him. He sits at the couch and starts putting pieces in place. Grammy enters.)*
GRAMMY. Made some phone calls. *(She crosses to the puzzle as well, compelled, like Bill, to continue piecing it together. Lisa enters from the kitchen carrying a plate with toast on it. She takes it up to Tami, who shakes her head "no.")*
LISA. Grammy, Dad — toast? *(They shake their heads "no," and Lisa sits at the table and eats the toast.)*
GRAMMY. *(To Bill.)* Maybe we should take this to the funeral home and let everyone finish it?
BILL. Oh...? Well ... that sounds like a good idea. *(They stop working on the puzzle.)*

GRAMMY. *(To Tami.)* Tami?

TAMI. *(Turning away from her screen to face them.)* Huh?

GRAMMY. The puzzle … I thought maybe we should take it and let people help finish it. Then we could shellac it and put it up in his room … .Or, well … somewhere.

TAMI. His teacher might like it for the classroom.

GRAMMY. Sure.

TAMI. I've sent out the emails. We need to figure out the service … *(The doorbell rings. Tami crosses to the door and opens it. A young man steps in [played by the same actor who played Josh]. This is Lawrence, a case-worker with DCFS.)*

LAWRENCE. Mrs. Martin? *(Tami nods — he hands her a card.)* I'm Lawrence Malerry with the Department of Child and Family Services. May I come in for a moment? *(Bill crosses up to them.)*

BILL. Can I help you? *(Tami closes the door behind Lawrence.)*

LAWRENCE. I'm very sorry for your loss, Mr. and Mrs. Martin. This is standard procedure when a child in the system dies under sus — dies in his home. I have a few questions for you and for the other child living here.

BILL. Oh, well … please come and sit down … *(He gestures to the dining table. Lisa moves near the computer as they sit.)*

GRAMMY. *(Moving toward the hallway.)* I'll get back on the phone, let you talk …

LAWRENCE. *(Opening his bag and pulling out a notebook.)* Okay. Just need to verify some details to make sure we have everything right in his file. Joshua was 18 years old?

BILL. Yes.

LAWRENCE. You were his legal guardians.

BILL. Yes.

LAWRENCE. And this was his primary residence.

BILL. Yes.

LAWRENCE. Is he on waiting lists for any homes? We'll need to release those positions if …

TAMI. No waiting lists.

LAWRENCE. Okay. *(He shifts to another piece of paper.)* First, was staff on duty last night?

TAMI. No.

LAWRENCE. And who was home with him?

TAMI. All of us, uh, and his grandma.

LAWRENCE. *(Nodding, writing.)* I am sorry to have to be both-

ering you with these questions. Now, Joshua's death was an accidental choking on popcorn?
BILL. Yes.
LAWRENCE. And did he have any history of breathing problems?
BILL. No.
LAWRENCE. Was he often left alone while eating?
TAMI. What kind of a question is that?
LAWRENCE. I'm simply ...
BILL. It's okay. Let him do his job. Yes, he often ate in his room, alone, and there had never been any problems prior to this.
LAWRENCE. Of course, and I'm sorry, Mrs. Martin, if these questions seem ...
BILL. It's fine.
LAWRENCE. I'm required to ask about these things. May I speak to *(He looks at notes.)* Lisa?
LISA. I'm here.
BILL. *(Gesturing to her.)* Come here and answer his questions. *(Lisa moves to sit next to Lawrence. As she's coming over, he takes a business card out of his file and has it in his hand.)*
LAWRENCE. I am sorry for the loss of your brother.
LISA. Sure.
LAWRENCE. And how are you doing? I mean, dealing with, the loss?
LISA. Fine.
LAWRENCE. I need to ask you a question, and if you'd like, we can speak privately.
LISA. What? No, I'm fine here.
LAWRENCE. Yes, but so you know, *(Handing her the business card.)* we can, speak privately, if you would ever want to.
LISA. *(Pushing it back to him, giving him a thumbs up.)* It's okay.
LAWRENCE. Fine. I need to know if you feel safe in this house. *(Lisa looks at her dad, back to Lawrence, and then bursts out laughing.)*
BILL. Lisa!?
LISA. *(Trying to control her laughter.)* I'm sorry, Dad, it's just ... I'm so much more safer NOW than before Josh died.
LAWRENCE. What?
LISA. Where were you for the past few years?
TAMI. Stop ...
LISA. What? You know it's true.
LAWRENCE. I'm afraid I don't understand.
LISA. No more Peanut Butter and Jelly for us! Woo hoo! *(She runs*

up and grabs Tami's hands and pulls them under the feathers. She dumps them on their heads, and they both start to laugh. Tami begins to jump and laugh with Lisa, spinning around until they both fall down. Their laughter dies down to silence. An awkward silence.)
TAMI. *(Coming up from behind the couch, her head peering over.)* That was inappropriate.
LISA. Mom — it's so not!
BILL. Are you okay?
TAMI. I'm not sure. *(A beat.)* That did feel good, Lisa.
LISA. OK. I get why you need to act sad about this, but come on. He's gone now and we don't have to be scared all the time.
TAMI. We're not "acting" sad.
LISA. We can go on vacations together. You can both come to my school stuff At The Same Time! Come on, Mom — I know you get it.
LAWRENCE. *(Standing.)* I, uh, well, I think I have what I need for my report. *(Less formally.)* That feather-falling thing is really interesting. *(Lisa crosses back to her toast while Bill starts picking up the feathers.)*
TAMI. *(Moving to Lawrence.)* Josh loved it. He would do this — kind of — happy dance.
LAWRENCE. Happy dance?
TAMI. Yeah. *(She looks at Lawrence, then shows him what Josh's happy dance looked like. Lawrence joins her, doing a remarkably accurate version of the dance. Tami is puzzled. Neither Bill or Lisa see this interchange.)*
BILL. *(To Lisa.)* Help me finish with the feathers?
LISA. *(Rolling her eyes.)* Let me at least finish my breakfast. *(Lisa takes her plate of toast and exits to the kitchen.)*
LAWRENCE. Anyway, thank you for your time, and here's my card — *(As he pulls his wallet out of his pocket, three marbles fall to the floor.)* Oops! Sorry about that. *(Tami picks up the marbles.)*
TAMI. It's okay. *(Handing him back the marbles.)* You have marbles?
LAWRENCE. *(Laughing.)* It's a weird hobby, I know. I collect marbles, and this morning a friend …
TAMI. … gave you marbles?
LAWRENCE. She found them in a jar at this estate auction and thought they might be …
TAMI. Josh loved marbles.
LAWRENCE. Oh. *(Putting the marbles in his pocket.)* I apologize if this …
BILL. No, it's fine.

TAMI. I didn't know it was a grown-up hobby.
BILL. *(As he puts the dining chair back.)* He has this huge marble run — would you like to see it?
LAWRENCE. *(A big grin.)* Really? That would be great! I've been designing my own marble run.
BILL. Come on.
LAWRENCE. *(Leaving with Bill — his voice and movements begin to slightly resemble Josh's.)* It has three different tornado slides and a pulley that automatically takes the marbles back to the top so it ... *(Bill and Lawrence exit as Tami crosses to sit on the couch. She makes the same "overwhelmed" gesture that she did previously, and there's an abrupt shift of light back to the way it was before the "Call 911" dialogue. We hear the same children's song coming from Josh's room. Tami looks up with a realization.)*
TAMI. Josh? *(Lisa sticks her head through the kitchen door.)*
LISA. Is there ice cream?
TAMI. What?
LISA. To go with the pie?
TAMI. The pie?
LISA. *(Stepping into the room, waving a pie server she is carrying.)* That was one of my choices, right? To get dessert ready?
TAMI. Yeah. Wait.
LISA. What?
TAMI. *(Remembering.)* You wanted to go live with Grammy. Then you went to get the pie.
LISA. Well, I don't really want to live with her.
TAMI. Oh. *(Bill enters from hallway. Children's music continues to play from Josh's room.)*
BILL. Josh wants *Curious George Goes to the Hospital* — have you seen it? *(Tami stands, confused.)*
LISA. *(To Bill.)* I think it's on the kitchen counter.
BILL. Thanks. *(He crosses to the kitchen door and exits.)*
LISA. *(Crossing to Tami.)* Mom? You okay? *(Tami grabs Lisa's hand.)*
TAMI. Josh is ... where?
LISA. In his room, I guess — Dad's getting the book ...
TAMI. He is?
LISA. *Curious George* — the hospital — what he just said...?
TAMI. Oh. *(She starts to cry.)*
LISA. What? *Curious George* is okay. Remember — he has an oper-

ation and makes the little girl laugh. *(Tami starts to laugh.)* OK. Many weird points on the mom scale today.

TAMI. I was thinking that ...

LISA. Yeah?

TAMI. Never mind. You don't want to go with Grammy?

LISA. I want to get away, but ... *(Tami suddenly hugs Lisa tightly to her. Bill enters with the book, but stops when he sees Lisa being held so tightly by Tami.)*

BILL. *(To Lisa.)* You okay?

LISA. *(An attempt to return Mom to normalcy.)* Should I make some lemonade? Or does Grammy want coffee? *(Tami doesn't respond, still trying to sort out what happened.)*

BILL. Why don't you go ask her. *(Tami lets go of Lisa, who exits to the hallway. Bill stays where he is. Tami moves to him, maybe reaching out to touch him.)*

TAMI. *(Somewhat frantic.)* I had this strange, I don't know what — I thought Josh was dead. And there was a man, he worked for Family Services. He collected marbles.

BILL. *(A little concerned.)* Okay ...

TAMI. I dreamt that Josh was dead, and I thought maybe I really do want him dead. How awful is that? I really don't.

BILL. I know you don't.

TAMI. I don't know what it means!

BILL. Dreams are crazy.

TAMI. When he was gone ... I felt so ...

BILL. Relieved? *(On her reaction.)* Guilty?

TAMI. No. Nothing. It's like everything was dead. I think ... I think it means that I don't want Josh to go away. He shouldn't live somewhere else.

BILL. Well not right now, but someday.

TAMI. No! I don't want to send him away.

BILL. What?

TAMI. He'll think we don't love him anymore.

BILL. We'd still see him. He just wouldn't be here all the time.

TAMI. It's too scary.

BILL. No, the idea of living in fear for the rest of my life is too scary.

TAMI. I'm always going to be scared for Josh, whether he's here or somewhere else. I choose this fear.

BILL. And if I don't agree?

TAMI. I don't know. *(We hear Lisa and Grammy as they enter from*

the hallway, laughing.)
GRAMMY. ... was so cute sipping his little cup with the rest of us!
LISA. Mom — Grammy was telling me about the "pretend coffee" she used to make for Dad when he was growing up. It was really just milk and sugar with, like, a drop of actual coffee in it, right?
GRAMMY. *(Teasing Bill.)* But he felt so grown-up when he drank it! Isn't that right?
JOSH. *(From his bedroom.)* Dad, help me. *Curious George*.
BILL. Saved by the book. *(Bill exits to take the book to Josh.)*
LISA. I wish I had a picture of Dad with his little coffee cup!
GRAMMY. I wish I had some "real coffee," please.
LISA. I'll go make some.
TAMI. Thanks, Lisa. *(Lisa exits to kitchen.)*
GRAMMY. Tami?
TAMI. Yeah?
GRAMMY. I really do want to be helpful. I just think that prayer is a good start.
TAMI. I know. It is.
GRAMMY. There must be something I can do to help ... Make some phone calls, or ... *(Grammy stops because she sees Bill entering.)*
BILL. Oh, sorry to interrupt.
GRAMMY. I was just telling Tami that I really do want to help.
BILL. I know you do, Mom. I'm sorry about earlier.
GRAMMY. You know, I've been having so much fun talking with Lisa, it made me think that — Well, maybe once my house sells I could move up here and be near you. Not to be in the way. But then Lisa could visit.
BILL. That would be nice.
GRAMMY. And maybe you could teach me how to help with Josh?
BILL. Well, maybe. I mean, I'm sure there are things you can do.
(Lisa sticks her head out of the kitchen.)
LISA. The coffee is dripping.
GRAMMY. Well, bless your heart.
LISA. Ready for some pie?
GRAMMY. Oh yes! *(Grammy exits to the kitchen as Lisa asks.)*
LISA. One scoop of ice cream or two?
GRAMMY. *(In the kitchen.)* Better just do one. Then I can have more later!
BILL. *(Picking up where their previous conversation left off.)* Well?
TAMI. Look, everything's a mess now because she's visiting. Once

she goes back home we'll get back on track.
BILL. That's what I'm afraid of.
TAMI. Hey, if this is too tough for you …
BILL. What? You want to be a single parent for Josh?
TAMI. No, of course not, but …
BILL. Tami, the only "track" we're on is headed for disaster.
TAMI. Thanks.
BILL. I'm not criticizing you.
TAMI. I think you are.
BILL. I have to believe there is help out there if you'd just trust someone.
TAMI. What? I haven't been working hard enough?
BILL. I don't know. You keep me out of the loop so …
TAMI. I keep you out of the loop because you want me to. It's easier that way.
BILL. Now I'm lazy, great. *(Josh enters with a large box of marbles, laughing. He runs to the dining room table and starts counting his marbles. The rest of their conversation is still emotionally intense, but now they have to mask it in some way so that Josh won't be upset by their voices.)*
TAMI. Lots of adults live with their parents.
BILL. Lots of adults aren't Josh.
TAMI. All the more reason for him to stay here.
BILL. How is it better for Josh if we're the only ones who can take care of him?
TAMI. How is it better for Josh if he's someplace where nobody loves him?
BILL. I know it's gonna be a long process, but we've got to move forward.
TAMI. *(Moving down toward the spot she was when she talked with Lawrence earlier.)* It just feels wrong. *(Exactly the same way as Lawrence did, Josh drops three marbles.)*
JOSH. Oops. Sorry 'bout that! *(Tami picks up the marbles.)*
TAMI. *(Automatically.)* It's okay. *(As she gives the marbles to Josh, she is struck by the déjà vu of this scene happening earlier with Lawrence. Tami draws an audible breath.)* Oh. It's not Josh …
BILL. What?
TAMI. *(Figuring it out as she goes.)* Who's dead. It's not Josh … It's the other one.
BILL. The other one …
TAMI. The man with the marbles. The one he could have been.

(Bill indicates his confusion with a gesture. Tami holds her stomach, remembering.) That dream — you know ... That he'll go to regular school and sing in the choir and go to college and get a job and be ... *(The grief hits her hard.)* It's dead. There's no dream for Josh.
JOSH. *(Reporting what he hears.)* Mom is crying. *(Tami draws a breath.)* Mom is sad.
TAMI. *(Struggling to make it so.)* Mommy is okay. Are you playing marbles?
BILL. You are not okay. We are not okay. *(A beat, maybe Tami moves or turns. Maybe Bill comes to her.)*
TAMI. Everything is falling apart.
BILL. I know.
TAMI. Can we fix it?
BILL. I don't know. Do you want to?
TAMI. I don't know.
LISA. *(From the kitchen.)* Hey, Dad, Mom — are you coming for pie?
BILL. In a minute.
TAMI. Go ahead.
BILL. Don't shut me out again.
TAMI. I'm not ... I just need to think.
BILL. OK. *(Bill exits. Tami crosses up to Josh.)*
TAMI. Joshy — give hugs? *(Josh stands and allows Tami to hug him for a second, then moves back to his marbles.)* Josh. Joshua William Martin. *(Lightly.)* Josh — help me — Mom is stuck.
JOSH. *(Echoing.)* Mom is stuck.
TAMI. *(Again with her playful voice.)* What will happen? *(No response from him. With a sigh.)* Oh, Josh. *(She moves down in front of the couch as he moves downstage with his hands full of marbles. She looks up and out. She speaks to the universe, to God, to anyone listening.)* Okay. Okay. *(Her breath catches — afraid, but taking the plunge.)* Catch me? *(She spreads her arms as Josh tosses the marbles in the air — they land and bounce all over the stage as Tami surrenders and falls back into the couch. Feathers fall on the audience. Josh squeals and does his most happy of dances. Lights fade to black.)*

End of Play

PROPERTY LIST

Laundry basket
Backpack, safety vest
Cup of coffee
Cell phones
Smoothie in glass
Empty food wrappers
Magic Marker
Backpack
Jacket or sweater
2 suitcases
Four-legged metal cane
Large purse with: wrapped gift, Baggie with pink sugar substitute packets, Bible, pillbox
Puzzle board
Mail
3 glasses of tea
Teaspoon
Notebook
Box of marbles
Wristwatch
TV remote
DVD
Paper and pen
Frozen strawberries
Glass of Shiraz wine
Plates, napkins, silverware
Glasses of water
Whiskey and 2 glasses
Large bowl popcorn
Plate with toast
Bag, notebook, papers, file
Business card
3 marbles
Pie server
Curious George book

SOUND EFFECTS

Blender, off
Car horn, off
Rock song from PC speaker
Cell phone ring
Buzzer sound, off
TV dialog, then superfast and high-pitched
Dog barking, off, then fade
Children's music video, off
Children's cartoon
Dog barking, soft then louder
Sirens
Doorbell

NEW PLAYS

★ MOTHERHOOD OUT LOUD by Leslie Ayvazian, Brooke Berman, David Cale, Jessica Goldberg, Beth Henley, Lameece Issaq, Claire LaZebnik, Lisa Loomer, Michele Lowe, Marco Pennette, Theresa Rebeck, Luanne Rice, Annie Weisman and Cheryl L. West, conceived by Susan R. Rose and Joan Stein. When entrusting the subject of motherhood to such a dazzling collection of celebrated American writers, what results is a joyous, moving, hilarious, and altogether thrilling theatrical event. "Never fails to strike both the funny bone and the heart." —*BackStage.* "Packed with wisdom, laughter, and plenty of wry surprises." —*TheaterMania.* [1M, 3W] ISBN: 978-0-8222-2589-8

★ COCK by Mike Bartlett. When John takes a break from his boyfriend, he accidentally meets the girl of his dreams. Filled with guilt and indecision, he decides there is only one way to straighten this out. "[A] brilliant and blackly hilarious feat of provocation." —*Independent.* "A smart, prickly and rewarding view of sexual and emotional confusion." —*Evening Standard.* [3M, 1W] ISBN: 978-0-8222-2766-3

★ F. Scott Fitzgerald's THE GREAT GATSBY adapted for the stage by Simon Levy. Jay Gatsby, a self-made millionaire, passionately pursues the elusive Daisy Buchanan. Nick Carraway, a young newcomer to Long Island, is drawn into their world of obsession, greed and danger. "Levy's combination of narration, dialogue and action delivers most of what is best in the novel." —*Seattle Post-Intelligencer.* "A beautifully crafted interpretation of the 1925 novel which defined the Jazz Age." —*London Free Press.* [5M, 4W] ISBN: 978-0-8222-2727-4

★ LONELY, I'M NOT by Paul Weitz. At an age when most people are discovering what they want to do with their lives, Porter has been married and divorced, earned seven figures as a corporate "ninja," and had a nervous breakdown. It's been four years since he's had a job or a date, and he's decided to give life another shot. "Critic's pick!" —*NY Times.* "An enjoyable ride." —*NY Daily News.* [3M, 3W] ISBN: 978-0-8222-2734-2

★ ASUNCION by Jesse Eisenberg. Edgar and Vinny are not racist. In fact, Edgar maintains a blog condemning American imperialism, and Vinny is three-quarters into a Ph.D. in Black Studies. When Asuncion becomes their new roommate, the boys have a perfect opportunity to demonstrate how open-minded they truly are. "Mr. Eisenberg writes lively dialogue that strikes plenty of comic sparks." —*NY Times.* "An almost ridiculously enjoyable portrait of slacker trauma among would-be intellectuals." —*Newsday.* [2M, 2W] ISBN: 978-0-8222-2630-7

DRAMATISTS PLAY SERVICE, INC.
440 Park Avenue South, New York, NY 10016 212-683-8960 Fax 212-213-1539
postmaster@dramatists.com www.dramatists.com

NEW PLAYS

★ **THE PICTURE OF DORIAN GRAY by Roberto Aguirre-Sacasa, based on the novel by Oscar Wilde.** Preternaturally handsome Dorian Gray has his portrait painted by his college classmate Basil Hallwood. When their mutual friend Henry Wotton offers to include it in a show, Dorian makes a fateful wish—that his portrait should grow old instead of him—and strikes an unspeakable bargain with the devil. [5M, 2W] ISBN: 978-0-8222-2590-4

★ **THE LYONS by Nicky Silver.** As Ben Lyons lies dying, it becomes clear that he and his wife have been at war for many years, and his impending demise has brought no relief. When they're joined by their children all efforts at a sentimental goodbye to the dying patriarch are soon abandoned. "Hilariously frank, clear-sighted, compassionate and forgiving." –*NY Times.* "Mordant, dark and rich." –*Associated Press.* [3M, 3W] ISBN: 978-0-8222-2659-8

★ **STANDING ON CEREMONY by Mo Gaffney, Jordan Harrison, Moisés Kaufman, Neil LaBute, Wendy MacLeod, José Rivera, Paul Rudnick, and Doug Wright, conceived by Brian Shnipper.** Witty, warm and occasionally wacky, these plays are vows to the blessings of equality, the universal challenges of relationships and the often hilarious power of love. "CEREMONY puts a human face on a hot-button issue and delivers laughter and tears rather than propaganda." –*BackStage.* [3M, 3W] ISBN: 978-0-8222-2654-3

★ **ONE ARM by Moisés Kaufman, based on the short story and screenplay by Tennessee Williams.** Ollie joins the Navy and becomes the lightweight boxing champion of the Pacific Fleet. Soon after, he loses his arm in a car accident, and he turns to hustling to survive. "[A] fast, fierce, brutally beautiful stage adaptation." –*NY Magazine.* "A fascinatingly lurid, provocative and fatalistic piece of theater." –*Variety.* [7M, 1W] ISBN: 978-0-8222-2564-5

★ **AN ILIAD by Lisa Peterson and Denis O'Hare.** A modern-day retelling of Homer's classic. Poetry and humor, the ancient tale of the Trojan War and the modern world collide in this captivating theatrical experience. "Shocking, glorious, primal and deeply satisfying." –*Time Out NY.* "Explosive, altogether breathtaking." –*Chicago Sun-Times.* [1M] ISBN: 978-0-8222-2687-1

★ **THE COLUMNIST by David Auburn.** At the height of the Cold War, Joe Alsop is the nation's most influential journalist, beloved, feared and courted by the Washington world. But as the '60s dawn and America undergoes dizzying change, the intense political dramas Joe is embroiled in become deeply personal as well. "Intensely satisfying." –*Bloomberg News.* [5M, 2W] ISBN: 978-0-8222-2699-4

DRAMATISTS PLAY SERVICE, INC.
440 Park Avenue South, New York, NY 10016   212-683-8960   Fax 212-213-1539
postmaster@dramatists.com   www.dramatists.com

NEW PLAYS

★ **BENGAL TIGER AT THE BAGHDAD ZOO by Rajiv Joseph.** The lives of two American Marines and an Iraqi translator are forever changed by an encounter with a quick-witted tiger who haunts the streets of war-torn Baghdad. "[A] boldly imagined, harrowing and surprisingly funny drama." –*NY Times.* "Tragic yet darkly comic and highly imaginative." –*CurtainUp.* [5M, 2W] ISBN: 978-0-8222-2565-2

★ **THE PITMEN PAINTERS by Lee Hall, inspired by a book by William Feaver.** Based on the triumphant true story, a group of British miners discover a new way to express themselves and unexpectedly become art-world sensations. "Excitingly ambiguous, in-the-moment theater." –*NY Times.* "Heartfelt, moving and deeply politicized." –*Chicago Tribune.* [5M, 2W] ISBN: 978-0-8222-2507-2

★ **RELATIVELY SPEAKING by Ethan Coen, Elaine May and Woody Allen.** In TALKING CURE, Ethan Coen uncovers the sort of insanity that can only come from family. Elaine May explores the hilarity of passing in GEORGE IS DEAD. In HONEYMOON MOTEL, Woody Allen invites you to the sort of wedding day you won't forget. "Firecracker funny." –*NY Times.* "A rollicking good time." –*New Yorker.* [8M, 7W] ISBN: 978-0-8222-2394-8

★ **SONS OF THE PROPHET by Stephen Karam.** If to live is to suffer, then Joseph Douaihy is more alive than most. With unexplained chronic pain and the fate of his reeling family on his shoulders, Joseph's health, sanity, and insurance premium are on the line. "Explosively funny." –*NY Times.* "At once deep, deft and beautifully made." –*New Yorker.* [5M, 3W] ISBN: 978-0-8222-2597-3

★ **THE MOUNTAINTOP by Katori Hall.** A gripping reimagination of events the night before the assassination of the civil rights leader Dr. Martin Luther King, Jr. "An ominous electricity crackles through the opening moments." –*NY Times.* "[A] thrilling, wild, provocative flight of magical realism." –*Associated Press.* "Crackles with theatricality and a humanity more moving than sainthood." –*NY Newsday.* [1M, 1W] ISBN: 978-0-8222-2603-1

★ **ALL NEW PEOPLE by Zach Braff.** Charlie is 35, heartbroken, and just wants some time away from the rest of the world. Long Beach Island seems to be the perfect escape until his solitude is interrupted by a motley parade of misfits who show up and change his plans. "Consistently and sometimes sensationally funny." –*NY Times.* "A morbidly funny play about the trendy new existential condition of being young, adorable, and miserable." –*Variety.* [2M, 2W] ISBN: 978-0-8222-2562-1

DRAMATISTS PLAY SERVICE, INC.
440 Park Avenue South, New York, NY 10016 212-683-8960 Fax 212-213-1539
postmaster@dramatists.com   www.dramatists.com

NEW PLAYS

★ **CLYBOURNE PARK by Bruce Norris.** WINNER OF THE 2011 PULITZER PRIZE AND 2012 TONY AWARD. Act One takes place in 1959 as community leaders try to stop the sale of a home to a black family. Act Two is set in the same house in the present day as the now predominantly African-American neighborhood battles to hold its ground. "Vital, sharp-witted and ferociously smart." *–NY Times.* "A theatrical treasure…Indisputably, uproariously funny." *–Entertainment Weekly.* [4M, 3W] ISBN: 978-0-8222-2697-0

★ **WATER BY THE SPOONFUL by Quiara Alegría Hudes.** WINNER OF THE 2012 PULITZER PRIZE. A Puerto Rican veteran is surrounded by the North Philadelphia demons he tried to escape in the service. "This is a very funny, warm, and yes uplifting play." *–Hartford Courant.* "The play is a combination poem, prayer and app on how to cope in an age of uncertainty, speed and chaos." *–Variety.* [4M, 3W] ISBN: 978-0-8222-2716-8

★ **RED by John Logan.** WINNER OF THE 2010 TONY AWARD. Mark Rothko has just landed the biggest commission in the history of modern art. But when his young assistant, Ken, gains the confidence to challenge him, Rothko faces the agonizing possibility that his crowning achievement could also become his undoing. "Intense and exciting." *–NY Times.* "Smart, eloquent entertainment." *–New Yorker.* [2M] ISBN: 978-0-8222-2483-9

★ **VENUS IN FUR by David Ives.** Thomas, a beleaguered playwright/director, is desperate to find an actress to play Vanda, the female lead in his adaptation of the classic sadomasochistic tale *Venus in Fur*. "Ninety minutes of good, kinky fun." *–NY Times.* "A fast-paced journey into one man's entrapment by a clever, vengeful female." *–Associated Press.* [1M, 1W] ISBN: 978-0-8222-2603-1

★ **OTHER DESERT CITIES by Jon Robin Baitz.** Brooke returns home to Palm Springs after a six-year absence and announces that she is about to publish a memoir dredging up a pivotal and tragic event in the family's history—a wound they don't want reopened. "Leaves you feeling both moved and gratifyingly sated." *–NY Times.* "A genuine pleasure." *–NY Post.* [2M, 3W] ISBN: 978-0-8222-2605-5

★ **TRIBES by Nina Raine.** Billy was born deaf into a hearing family and adapts brilliantly to his family's unconventional ways, but it's not until he meets Sylvia, a young woman on the brink of deafness, that he finally understands what it means to be understood. "A smart, lively play." *–NY Times.* "[A] bright and boldly provocative drama." *–Associated Press.* [3M, 2W] ISBN: 978-0-8222-2751-9

DRAMATISTS PLAY SERVICE, INC.
440 Park Avenue South, New York, NY 10016 212-683-8960 Fax 212-213-1539
postmaster@dramatists.com www.dramatists.com